THE BUILDINGS OF BYZANTIUM

Helen and Richard Leacroft

HODDER & STOUGHTON
LONDON LEICESTER SYDNEY AUCKLAND
and
ADDISON-WESLEY PUBLISHING COMPANY

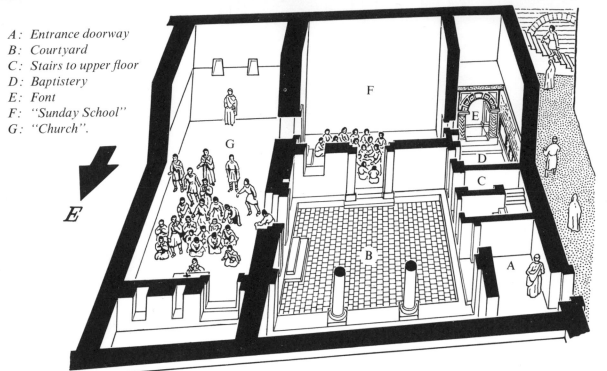

A: Entrance doorway
B: Courtyard
C: Stairs to upper floor
D: Baptistery
E: Font
F: "Sunday School"
G: "Church".

CHRISTIAN COMMUNITY HOUSE,
Dura-Europos, Iraq. c. A.D. 230.

BYZANTIUM, the city founded by the Greek, Byzaz, in the seventh century B.C., stood on a peninsula of land at the entrance to the Bosphorus (page 39), and was at the crossroads of eastern and western civilizations. By the third century A.D., it had developed into a typical Roman city. It was therefore the ideal place for Constantine the Great to develop as his new capital, when he became the ruler of the Eastern Roman Empire. The power of Rome had declined in the third century A.D. One reason for this was that barbarians were constantly attacking the frontiers; another was that there were no rules laid down regarding who should succeed an emperor when he died, so any powerful commander could march on Rome and set himself up as a ruler. It was Emperor Diocletian, A.D. 284–305, who, in an effort to strengthen the rule of law, decided that the Empire was too large for one man to control, so he divided it into two parts, the West and the East. When he died, however, fighting broke out again, and it was Constantine who restored order in the East. Declaring that he ruled by the will of God, and allying himself with the Christian Church, he dedicated his Empire on 11 May, A.D. 330, in the city of Byzantium, later to be called Constantinople, and now known as Istanbul.

Most of the Byzantine buildings which can still be seen today are churches, many richly decorated with mosaics. But the Byzantines also built palaces, basilicas, hospitals and markets which were all essential to a great trading nation, whose culture was to have such an effect on our western world.

EARLY CHRISTIAN CHURCHES

Early Christian groups in many towns and villages were often small. They did not build special churches, but gathered to worship in private houses, which were adapted for use by the communities. Another reason for using this type of building may have been that, before Constantine's Edict of Milan in A.D. 313 which allowed people to worship as they wished, Christians suffered periods of persecution from the Roman emperors, and it was not advisable for them to advertise their presence. The remains of such a private 'church' house – *domus ecclesiae* – have been excavated at Dura-Europos, a Roman legionary fortress in Iraq. As well as a room converted into a church, two other essential features were found – a baptistery and a font.

When Christianity became the official religion of Constantine's empire, churches had to be built. In the ancient world the pagan temples were the homes of the gods, and people did not enter but worshipped in sacred spaces before the buildings. Christians, however, needed a place in which they could meet together for their worship, discussions and teaching, and they used the form of building developed by the Romans for their public gatherings – the basilica. An example of a basilican-type of church may be seen in S. Clemente. The semi-circular apse contained the bishop's throne – *cathedra* – and seating for the elders. A railed-off portion of the nave in front of the apse was used by the clergy, while the congregation stood around the sides.

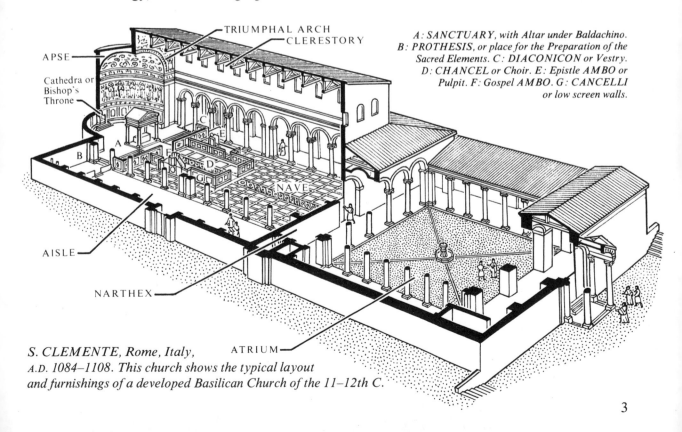

APSE

Cathedra or Bishop's Throne

TRIUMPHAL ARCH
CLERESTORY

A: SANCTUARY, with Altar under Baldachino.
B: PROTHESIS, or place for the Preparation of the Sacred Elements. C: DIACONICON or Vestry.
D: CHANCEL or Choir. E: Epistle AMBO or Pulpit. F: Gospel AMBO. G: CANCELLI
or low screen walls.

NAVE

AISLE

NARTHEX

S. CLEMENTE, Rome, Italy,
ATRIUM
A.D. 1084–1108. This church shows the typical layout and furnishings of a developed Basilican Church of the 11–12th C.

A TYPICAL BASILICAN CHURCH
was divided into three aisles, with a raised apse
covered by a semi-dome at the eastern end; this
sometimes projected beyond the building or
could be completely enclosed by it. The central
aisle or nave was usually broader and higher
than the side aisles and was lit by windows in a
'clear storey' – *clerestory* – which was supported on columns linked by round-headed
arches. The building was covered by a pitched
timber and tiled roof.

The position of the altar varied from church
to church. It could be sited against the rear wall
of the apse, as was often to be found in the
Byzantine churches of Syria, or at the edge of
the steps as seen above. Altars were also placed
below the steps (page 8), or even in the middle
of a domed sanctuary. The celebration of the
Mass was secret so it could not be viewed by the
congregation. The altar was therefore often
covered by a canopy supported on columns –
baldachino – and curtains were drawn around it

when the bread and wine were consecrated during the service. The clergy took their places within the railings – *chancels* – and in some churches the whole nave was used for processions which formed an important part of the services. The pulpit – *ambo* – was used for sermons and the reading of the gospels, and was usually to be found by one of the chancel rails, but sometimes it was placed farther down the nave. Later, separate pulpits were provided, one for the reading of the gospel and one for the epistle, as at S. Clemente (page 3) and above as shown in the illustration.

The lower walls were covered with marble, and the upper walls glistened with mosaics. As most of the congregation could not read, these mosaic pictures were used to teach them the Bible stories. The mosaics also depicted saints, and the martyrs who had died for their Christian faith; all leading up to a view of Paradise or Christ in Glory (page 9) set in the semi-dome of the half-round apse.

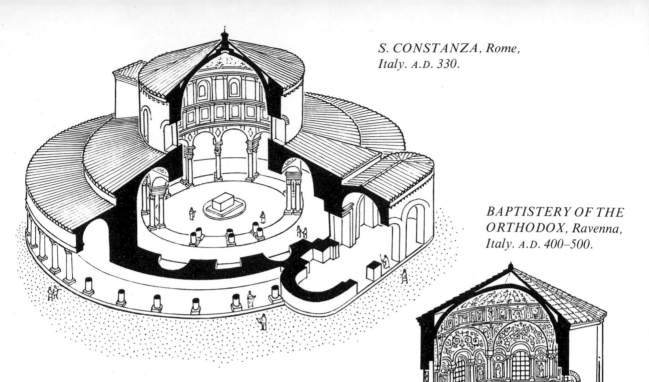

S. CONSTANZA, Rome, Italy. A.D. 330.

BAPTISTERY OF THE ORTHODOX, Ravenna, Italy. A.D. 400–500.

When a Roman emperor died the people believed that he became one of the gods, and a temple was dedicated to his memory where offerings could be made. When Constantine adopted Christianity he realised that it would be impossible to overthrow all pagan ideas immediately, and so he kept and adapted such beliefs and buildings as could be used by the new faith. The Roman basilica was at first found to be suitable for communal Christian worship, and the Roman funerary temple developed into the emperor's mausoleum or tomb. Constantine did not, of course, suggest that he became one with God but, nevertheless, he expected his tomb and those of his family to become shrines to which people would come as pilgrims. Other holy sanctuaries were the tombs where the relics of the martyrs were buried. A circular building was found to be the type best suited to the requirements of the pilgrims. Here they could stand in circles around the central feature, the sarcophagus, a marble or stone coffin, and view it with ease. Such a building may still be seen today in the church of S. Constanza in Rome (see above). Originally built by Constantine as a mausoleum for his daughter Constantina, it shows all the necessary elements. In the middle was the sarcophagus on to which light flooded from windows set high up in the walls of the drum which supported a dome, representing the universe. Around the central area an ambulatory, or walking way, was covered by vaulting on which can still be seen mosaics of the fourth century A.D., combining both Christian and pagan scenes of the wine harvest. The outside of the building was encircled by a colonnade flanking an entrance porch.

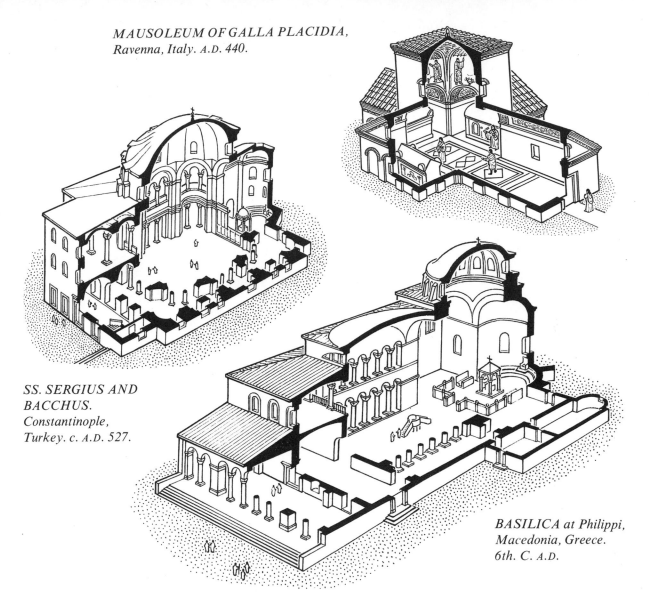

MAUSOLEUM OF GALLA PLACIDIA,
Ravenna, Italy. A.D. 440.

SS. SERGIUS AND
BACCHUS.
Constantinople,
Turkey. c. A.D. 527.

BASILICA at Philippi,
Macedonia, Greece.
6th. C. A.D.

As the crowds of pilgrims increased, shelter had to be provided for them, so the domed sanctuary was often placed next to, or incorporated within, a basilican-type church. An example of such a building was Constantine's rotunda covering the Holy Sepulchre in Jerusalem. Eusebius of Caesarea, an historian of the fourth century A.D., describes the mausoleum built for Constantine, who considered himself to be the thirteenth apostle, as being placed within the Church of the Holy Apostles in Constantinople. This church, set in a courtyard, was cross-shaped with the sarcophagus, flanked by piers, placed in the crossing beneath a drum covered by a dome.

There was usually only one baptistery in a town, and it was attached to the principal church. It was generally a circular or octagonal building. Here provision was made for many people as baptisms were carried out only three times a year, at Easter, Pentecost and Epiphany, the Feast of the Wise Men.

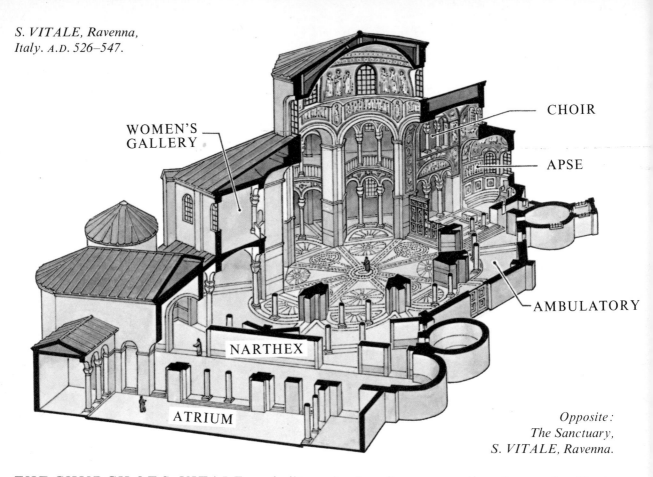

S. VITALE, Ravenna,
Italy. A.D. 526–547.

WOMEN'S GALLERY

CHOIR

APSE

AMBULATORY

NARTHEX

ATRIUM

Opposite:
The Sanctuary,
S. VITALE, Ravenna.

THE CHURCH OF S. VITALE was built by a rich banker for the Emperor Justinian, who reigned from A.D. 527–565. The main plan was similar to that of a circular mausoleum, for the services now included singing and the dome served to give resonance to the music. The space for the choir terminated in an apse and was separated from the nave, at first, perhaps by curtains in the manner shown in the illustration on the right, and later by a screen – *iconostasis* – which was covered with sacred pictures – *icons*.

Although the nave was greatly altered in Renaissance times, that is in the fourteenth and fifteenth centuries, the walls and ceiling of the apse are today still covered with the original mosaics. Above the triple window, Christ, with a nimbus or halo behind his head, is seated on a circular disc representing the earth. He is holding out a martyr's crown to S. Vitalis to whom the church is dedicated. On the right, a figure of a bishop carries a model of the church. It was the custom for the Byzantine emperor to have his portrait in the church, and that of Justinian, together with important church and civil dignitaries and guards, may be seen to the right of the window. On the wall opposite, the Empress Theodora (see endpapers) and her attendants are depicted. The mosaics show details of the rich fabrics and decorations. Further mosaics in the apse show Biblical scenes; the style of these is similar to the paintings of the Greeks, showing realistic landscape backgrounds such as are to be seen in S. Apollinare in Classe, Ravenna, but which were to disappear in later Byzantine decoration.

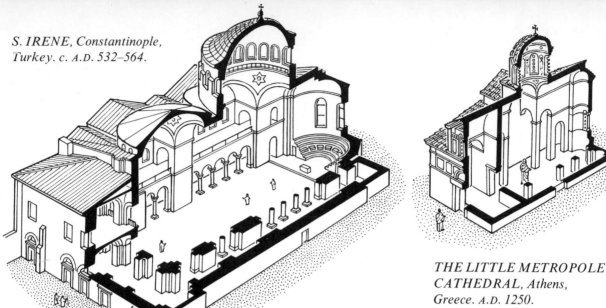

THE LITTLE METROPOLE CATHEDRAL, *Athens, Greece. A.D. 1250.*

The most difficult problem Byzantine builders had to overcome was how to support a dome. It was easy to build a circular dome over a circular plan as at S. Constanza (page 6), and comparatively simple when an octagonal shape was used as in the church of SS. Sergius and Bacchus at Constantinople (page 7), where eight piers linked by arches formed an octagon which supported the dome. It was, however, a different matter to put a dome over a square. The difficulty was resolved by the use of squinches and pendentives (see pages 14–15, and *The Buildings of Early Islam*, pages 14–15), which made it possible to turn a square into a circle. Once this method was discovered domes could be placed not only over a square space, but even the nave could be divided into bays each covered with a dome. The basilican church at Philippi (page 7) incorporated a high brick dome over the eastern end and a lower one over the nave. A similar arrangement may still be seen at S. Irene, Constantinople, where the nave is covered with two domes. One

reason for this change may have been that in the Eastern Empire timber for building was not plentiful; the early churches of Syria had to be roofed with solid stone slabs (page 35) in a manner similar to the temples of Ancient Egypt. The first church of S. Irene had been started in Byzantium before Constantine even came to the city, and until Hagia Sophia (see cover and pages 12–13) was built it may have been used as the cathedral. It was destroyed in the riots of A.D. 532. The present church, the third to be built, is, like that at Philippi, based on a basilican plan with a porch – *narthex* – a nave with aisles and a chancel with an apse.

The type which was to become the basic form of Byzantine church architecture was the 'cross in square'. The central area is covered by a dome carried on a high drum, which rests on a circle formed by pendentives, springing from four semi-circular arches, which were in turn supported by piers or columns at each corner of the square. The arches are extended as barrel vaults to the outer walls, so forming the arms of a cross. When this cross is fitted into a square building, the four small square corner bays which remain are covered, either with small domes or groined vaulting (see *The Buildings of Ancient Rome*, page 11), the whole forming a

10

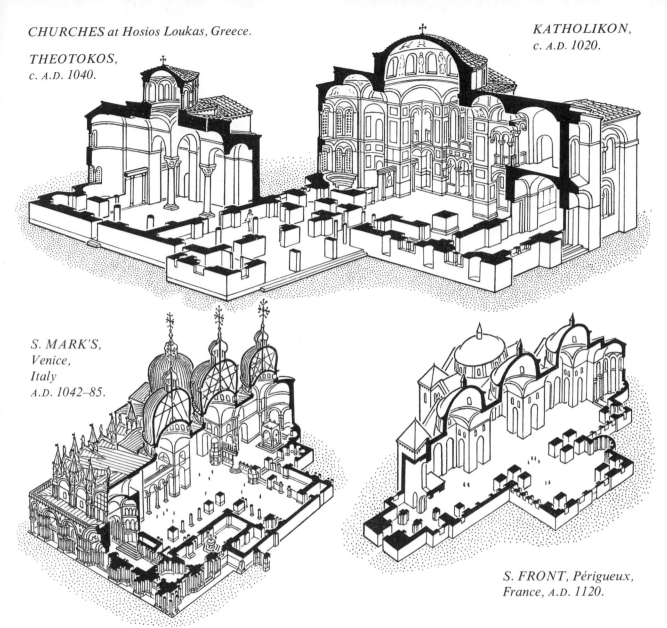

CHURCHES at Hosios Loukas, Greece.

THEOTOKOS,
c. A.D. 1040.

KATHOLIKON,
c. A.D. 1020.

S. MARK'S,
Venice,
Italy
A.D. 1042–85.

S. FRONT, Périgueux,
France, A.D. 1120.

building of nine bays. Another name for this type of building is *quincunx*.

The church of the Little Metropole, Athens, illustrates a stage in the development from basilica to 'cross in square', the aisles in this case being still clearly visible. The monastery churches of Hosios Loukas show how this plan could be elaborated and enlarged. In the small church of the Theotokos, the dome is sup-ported on four pillars set in a square, while in the larger Katholikon it is carried on an octagon on squinches.

The church of S. Mark's in Venice was modelled on the church of the Holy Apostles in Constantinople, but here each arm of the cross has its own dome. The influence which the Byzantine style had in western Europe may be seen in the church of S. Front in Périgueux.

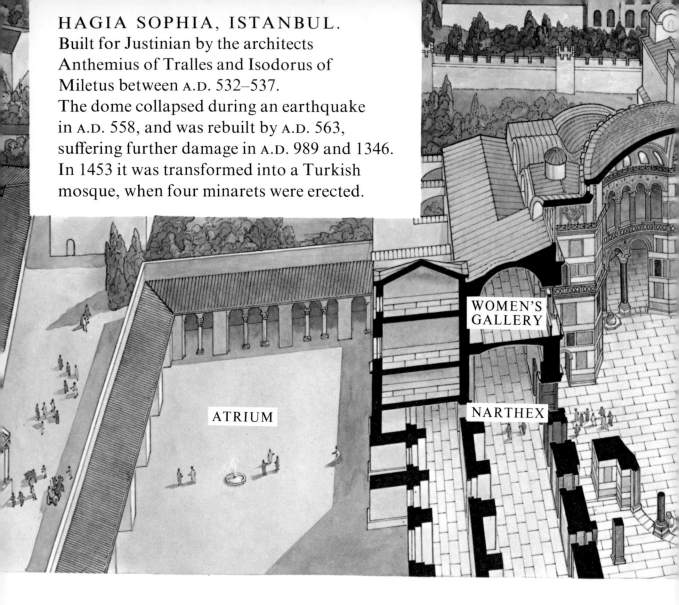

HAGIA SOPHIA, ISTANBUL.
Built for Justinian by the architects
Anthemius of Tralles and Isodorus of
Miletus between A.D. 532–537.
The dome collapsed during an earthquake
in A.D. 558, and was rebuilt by A.D. 563,
suffering further damage in A.D. 989 and 1346.
In 1453 it was transformed into a Turkish
mosque, when four minarets were erected.

WOMEN'S GALLERY

ATRIUM

NARTHEX

Hagia Sophia, the Holy Wisdom, was the principal church of the Byzantine world; its vast dome could be seen all over the city. Ten thousand workmen were employed on the building. Materials were brought from all parts of the empire, even the lead conduits of Constantinople were melted down to make coverings for the domes. Justinian came every day to supervise its progress. The basic plan was a basilica with a very wide nave, covered by a central dome. This was buttressed by half-domes on the east and west which roofed the spaces below. Beneath the great 'infilled' arches on the north and south, openings between the columns led into the aisles. To support the great weight a bed of concrete twenty feet (6.09 metres) thick was laid. The outer walls were built of brick, with holy relics buried at every twelfth course. The central dome was carried on massive piers of squared, smoothed, limestone, each stone being fastened in place with molten lead; the four pendentives which sup-

WOMEN'S GALLERY

EXEDRA

BEMA

APSE

AMBO

EXEDRA

SOUTH AISLE

ported it were each sixty feet (18.29 metres) in height. The square bricks for the domes were specially made in Rhodes. They were lighter than those used for the walls and varied in size. Each brick was stamped with the words "God founded this work and God will come to its aid."

Paul the Silentiary, an important official of Justinian's court wrote a poem describing the building. He said that when the first rosy light of morning, driving away the dark shadows, leaped from arch to arch, and the princes and people singing songs of prayer and praise came into the sacred areas, it seemed as if the mighty arches were set in heaven. At night a thousand lamps, hanging by chains, showed their gleaming lights, and through the spaces of the great church came rays of light expelling clouds of care and filling the mind with joy. The sailor on his dangerous course amidst rocks and creeks was guided safely into harbour by the twinkling of the lights which showed him not only the way to safety, but the way to the living God.

H. YOANNIS, Ligourio, Greece, c. A.D. 1080.

S. FOSCA, Torcello, Italy, c. A.D. 1008.

SQUINCHES AND PENDENTIVES

In early times man had learned to cover a building by placing layers of stones in circles, each layer of stones projecting slightly in front of the one below. This process of 'corbelling' was continued until a 'dome' had been constructed (see *The Buildings of Ancient Greece*, page 7). As already noted, it was easy enough to put a circular dome on a round building, but not so easy when the building was square. Some way had to be found to fill in the corners, and in a small building one simple solution was to place a stone slab across the corner angle of the walls, and then place further stones on top which corbelled out to cover the new angles until the square began to approach a straight-sided 'circle'. Another method which was used was to build an arch across the corner to support the upper slabs. As domes were made larger, additional small arches could be introduced arranged on one or more levels as at S. Fosca in Torcello, or a single large arch could be built across each corner containing what amounts to a vault in the form of a half dome, as may be seen at Daphni and in the Theotokos at Hosios Loukas (page 11). This arched vault construction was called a squinch.

CHURCH OF THE MONASTERY,
Daphni, Greece. A.D. 1080.

S. JOHN OF THE HERMITS,
Palermo, Sicily. A.D. 1132–48.

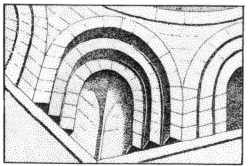

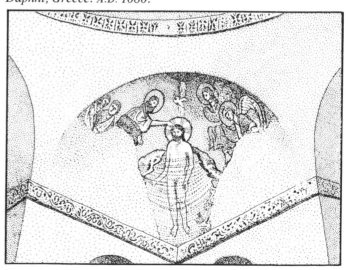

MAUSOLEUM OF GALLA PLACIDIA,
Ravenna, Italy. c. A.D. 440.

BAPTISTERY, S. MARK'S, Venice, Italy. A.D. 1042.

When a dome had to be placed over a square consisting of four large arches, the weight and downward thrust of even a light dome set on squinches would have tended to push the arches outwards so that they would have collapsed. The solution to the problem was the pendentive, which was a refinement of the corbelled stone slab construction described above. The pendentive was a curved triangle of shaped stones or bricks which was fitted in between the arches and rose up to form part of a low dome as at Galla Placidia, or until the four pendentives met to form a ring upon which a dome could be placed, in the same way that a lid fits on a jar. The Byzantines built largely in brick, and it was the use of this material which made it possible for them to bring the pendentive to perfection. To light the interior of the building the dome could be pierced with windows, but the builders found it easier to build these in a drum set upon the ring formed by the pendentives, with the dome built on top. This device helped to make the churches even higher and more imposing.

The idea of building a dome on pendentives was the greatest contribution which the Byzantines made to western architecture.

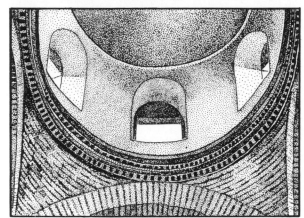

CONSTANTINE LIPS, NORTH CHURCH,
Constantinople, Turkey. A.D. 907.

S. SAVIOUR IN CHORA, Constantinople,
Turkey. c. 14th. C. A.D.

BUILDING A DOME. In the areas around Constantinople there was no stone of good quality for use in building. When stone was used it was imported, as were also the marbles for wall coverings and columns. These materials were expensive, and so brick and concrete were used for the main walls.

Scholars have suggested various ways in which domes were constructed; one may be seen in the illustration above. The pendentives have been built up to form a ring on which courses of thin flat bricks were laid in beds of mortar to form the dome, each course resting on the one beneath. To act as a guide to the required shape, timber ribs were set up spanning the opening, the width between each leg being the diameter of the inside of the dome. When all the bricks were in position the ribs were dismantled and removed.

Another method of setting out a dome was to use a trammel. This was a post set up vertically in the middle of the opening, level

16

with the top of the walls. Two poles were slotted over it so that they were free to be moved around in all directions. The length of the top pole was equal to the radius of the dome on its inner surface, and the bottom one measured the radius to the outside. When moved into position these rods set out exactly the thickness and rise of the dome. A further type of trammel had two rods which revolved around a central post, the whole forming a triangle. The top rod marked the slope of the dome, and when a course of bricks had to be laid, the rods were raised up on the central post to mark the position of the next course.

The master builders or architects – *mechanikos* – supervised the whole work, and groups of craftsmen – *technitai* – worked under them. Each craft was organised in a guild under a leader – *maistor* – and a council of craftsmen who were responsible for seeing that the workers were trained and that the work was of a high quality and standard.

BRONTOCHEION, Mistra, Greece.

S. PARASKEVI,
Mistra, Greece.

CONSTRUCTION AND DECORATION

Early Byzantine vaulting, making use of stone, concrete and brick, was similar to that used by the Romans, but later more use was made of thin shells of brick in the form of barrel or groin vaults. The roof of the great underground cistern of the Jere Batan (below) is made of bricks laid on edge with mortar between them; each of the four sections of the vault is shaped as a curved triangle meeting in the middle and being held in place by a key stone. Domes were built of brick, as shown on the previous pages, but to lighten the construction many domes, such as that of the Orthodox Baptistery in Ravenna, were built from hollow terracotta tubes which, as they were open at one end, could be interlocked to form a ring, each of which rested on the ring below.

The domes themselves were often covered with semicircular tiles of terracotta. The church of the monastery of the Brontocheion at Mistra (left) shows the way in which the tiles overlocked each other. The windows were narrow arched openings in the drum. A simple round-headed arch was constructed on timber centering, and further arches were built out from this until the thickness of the wall was reached. Sometimes the opening was filled with a round-headed pierced slab,

VAULT: JERE BATAN CISTERN
Constantinople, Turkey. 5th. C. A.D.

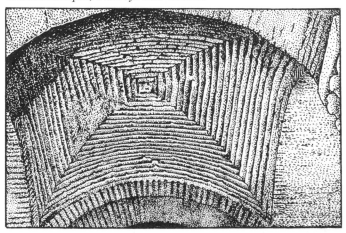

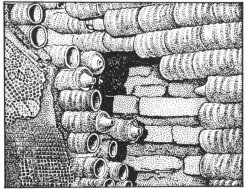

VAULTING: ORTHODOX BAPTISTERY.
Ravenna, Italy. c. A.D. 450.

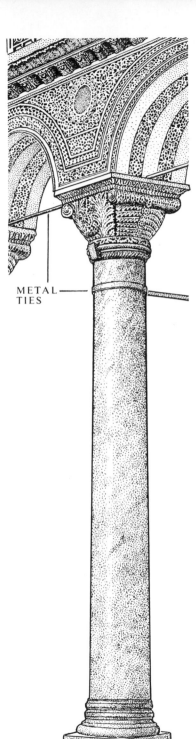

CAPITAL: S. LEONIDAS,
Corinth, Greece. c. A.D. 450.

CAPITAL: PHILIPPI BASILICA,
Macedonia, Greece. c. A.D. 540.

METAL—
TIES

which would have served as the centering for the first arch. As
domes and vaults were very light, they could be supported on thin
columns, with or without an impost. An impost was a stone
cushion, or half an inverted cone, which was placed between the
capital and the arch or vault that it supported; an example is
shown above from Philippi. By the sixth century the impost and
capital were often combined to form one unit, as at Hagia Sophia.
The skill of the Byzantine sculptors may be seen in the carving of
the acanthus leaves which formed the pattern on the capital. By
deep undercutting the design of white marble stood out from the
darker undersurface. Sometimes they pierced the leaves with
small holes to give light and shade. Often a cross or monogram
was carved in the middle of the leaves.

Inside the buildings, marble sheets were attached to the walls
by bronze clamps, while the outer walls were decorated by laying
the bricks in bands and patterns. Where masonry was used, bricks
were sometimes placed around each block of stone, either in
single or double courses; this type of work was called *cloisonné*, as
may be seen at S. Paraskevi (left).

WALL FINISHES. Left: Internal, Marble slabs fixed to
wall with bronze clamps. Right: External, use of stone and brick.

BRONZE
CLAMPS

H. SOPHIA. Constantinople,
Turkey. A.D. 532–537.

19

WATERWORKS.

The water supply for Constantinople came from the rivers and reservoirs in the hills beyond the city. It was carried down by means of aqueducts, and the people went to the public fountains to get their water. During the summer the flow dried up, so to make sure that there was a sufficient supply for everyday needs and for industry and agriculture, the emperors built vast underground cisterns where water could be stored when it was flowing freely. This provided an emergency supply in times of siege, and helped to prevent evaporation in hot weather.

The water was carried from the aqueducts into the cisterns in earthenware or lead pipes, which were also used to bring the supply to the public fountains, baths and the fonts of baptisteries. The cost of providing water came from the dues which the merchants paid for using the city wharves. All the services were under the control of the Praefectus Praetoria, the chief magistrate, who was also responsible for seeing that the canals carrying water to the fields were kept in order.

FONT AND PULPIT, ORTHODOX BAPTISTERY,
Ravenna, 5th. C. pulpit, medieval font.

UNDERGROUND CISTERN. BIN- BIR-DIREK, Constantinople, Turkey. 6th C. A.D.

BASILICA OF MAXENTIUS
& CONSTANTINE, Rome, Italy.
c. A.D. 300.

LAW AND POLITICS

In Rome basilicas were large halls where public business was transacted, agreements and contracts were signed, and where magistrates administered the justice to which all freemen were entitled. Such halls were also an important part of the official palace of the emperor, to whom appeal could be made if a man felt that he had not received justice in a lower court.

During his reign, Maxentius, emperor of Rome in A.D. 307–312, had started to build a vast basilica in that city (see *The Buildings of Ancient Rome*, page 20), which was altered and completed by Constantine before he set up his new capital at Constantinople, where he introduced the types of buildings to which he was accustomed. When the Romans developed the use of great vaults made of concrete, it became possible for them to change the form of the

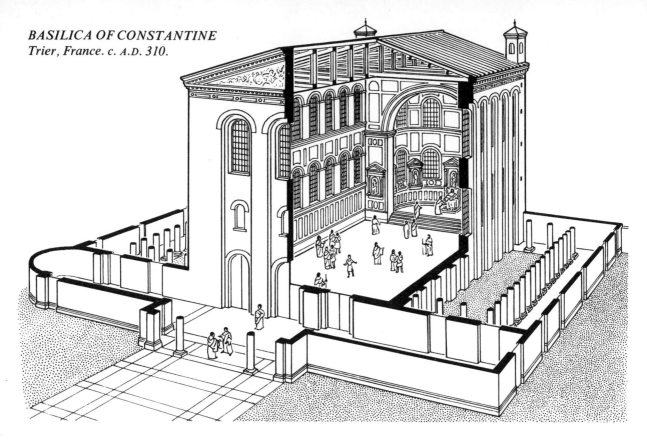

early basilicas with their long rows of columns, and cover them instead with several large vaults having their points of support at each corner. This arrangement set a precedent for the domed naves of churches (page 10). The aisles now became a series of interconnecting rectangles, separated from one another by cross-walls and from the nave by a single great arch. Each rectangular compartment was covered by a barrel vault. The walls were lined with slabs of coloured marble, and large windows in the arches of the nave vaults lit the great hall. In the apse, now at one end of the great nave, was the seat for the magistrate – *praetor* – the emperor's representative. A statue, or in later times a picture, of the emperor himself, was also always placed in the semi-circular apse.

The people who came for justice stood on the floor of the hall below the steps. While the magistrate was hearing legal cases or arguments, other business could be conducted in the compartments around the nave. In the palace basilica, the emperor's throne was placed in the apse with benches for high imperial officers set around the wall.

In the provinces of the Empire, the basilica was the headquarters of the administration. Although not so magnificent in appearance as the buildings of the capital, sometimes being a single nave without aisles as at Trier, the basilicas were sufficiently imposing to impress the native population with the might and power of their rulers. When the basilica became the pattern for the early Christian churches, the statue of the emperor, overseeing civil affairs, was replaced by a representation, in mosaic or fresco, of Christ as the Pantocrator, that is, as ruler of the world, holding a Bible in one hand and the other raised in blessing.

Towns

FORTIFIED TOWN:
from 6th. C. manuscript:
the Vienna Genesis.

ALEXANDRIA: from
a mosaic of A.D. 500.
Church of S. John,
Jerash, Transjordan

The geographical position of the Byzantine Empire (page 39) was such that it was surrounded by enemies and could be attacked from all sides. The towns, therefore, were fortified with walls and towers, and the great gates were closed at night to ensure the safety of the inhabitants. Such a town was Nicaea, shown below, but even the strength of these fortifications did not prevent its capture by the Crusaders in 1097.

Many of the town-dwellers were highly skilled craftsmen. Under the direction of the state they were obliged to manufacture the gold and silverware, the jewellery, vases and ornaments, and the rich brocades and damasks that were required by the Church, the Court and the wealthy owners of great estates. Such goods were also in demand by foreign countries, and so the wealth of the Byzantines depended upon a highly developed trade and commerce. Officials were needed to direct the production of goods and make sure that taxes were paid, and the quality approved. For example, any silk merchants who did not show to the magistrate goods which were to be exported to foreign countries, so that they could receive his official seal, were liable to be punished severely. There were many such regulations which had to be obeyed, and offices were needed where the officials could work. The state also built warehouses where the finished merchandise could be stored. Each particular craft was to be found in its own area in the town, working under the direction of a guild. Special quarters were set aside in Constantinople for foreign merchants, as may be seen in the illustration on the next page, numbers 19–23.

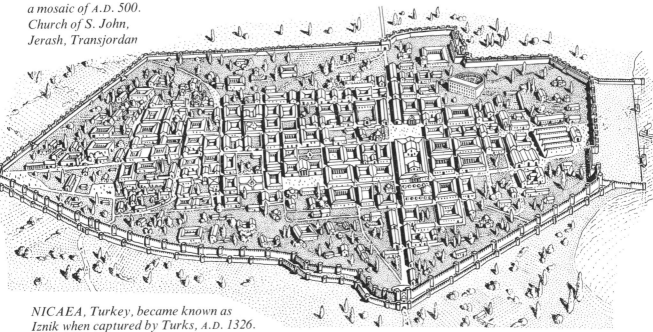

NICAEA, Turkey, became known as
Iznik when captured by Turks, A.D. 1326.

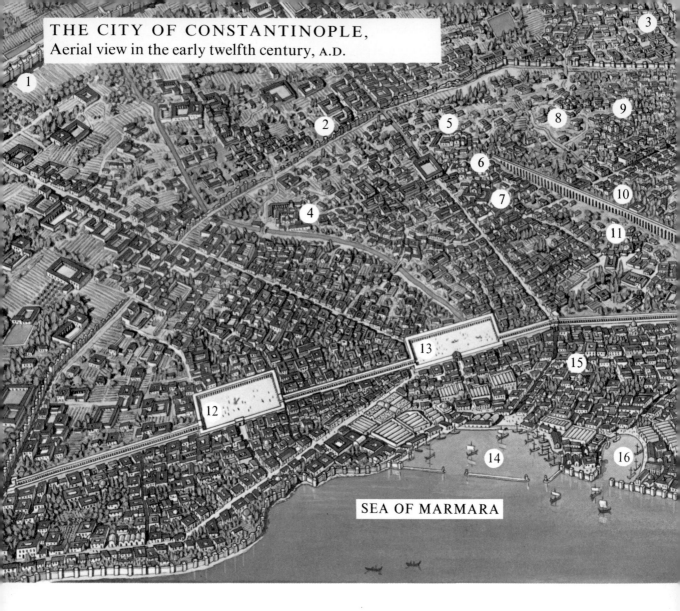

THE CITY OF CONSTANTINOPLE,
Aerial view in the early twelfth century, A.D.

SEA OF MARMARA

1. Walls of Theodosius.
2. Walls of Constantine.
3. Church of Theodora.
4. Monastery of Constantine Lips.
5. Church of the Holy Apostles.
6. Church of S. Christopher.
7. Monastery of S. Polyeuctes.
8. Church of Christ Pantopoptos.
9. Church of Christ Pantocrator.
10. Aqueduct of Valens.
11. Church of Christ Akataleptos.
12. Forum of Arcadius.
13. Forum of the Ox.
14. Harbour of Eleutherius.
15. Monastery of Myrelaion.
16. Harbour of Heptaskalon.
17. Monastery of S. Zachary.
18. Forum of Theodosius.
19. Quarter of the Egyptians.
20. Quarter of the Venetians.
21. Quarter of Amalfi.
22. Quarter of Pisa.
23. Quarter of Genoa.
24. Galata and tower of Anastasi
25. Great Colonnades of Domnin
26. Baths of Dagistheus.
27. Palace of Nicephorus 111.
28. Forum of Constantine.
29. Harbour of Kontoskalion.
30. Harbour of Julian.

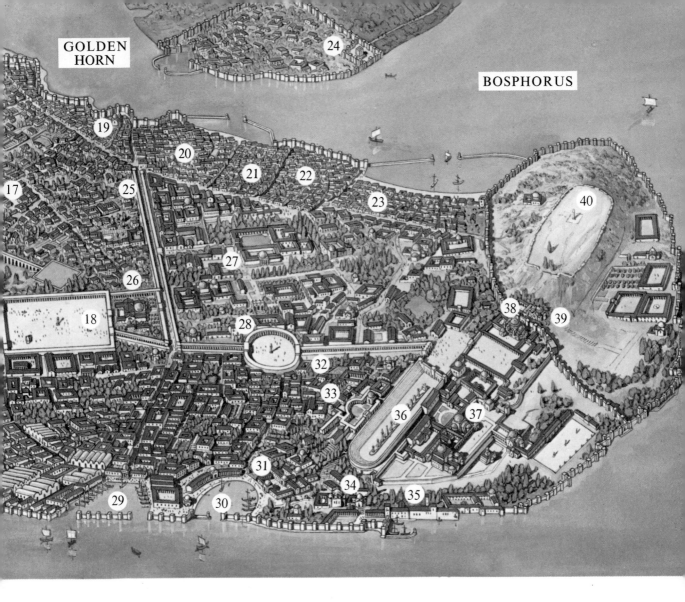

GOLDEN HORN

BOSPHORUS

. *Palace called Porphyra.*
. *Cistern of Philoxenus.*
. *Palace of Antioch.*
. *Church of SS. Sergius and Bacchus.*
. *Palaces of Bucoleon and Justinian 1.*
. *Hippodrome.*
. *Great Palace.*
. *Church of Hagia Sophia.*
. *Church of S. Irene.*
. *Acropolis. Ancient Greek.*

This illustration of Constantinople clearly shows the way in which the city developed over the centuries. Lined by colonnades to make shady walking ways, the main street – the *mese* – from which all other roads radiated, ran through the various fora which the early emperors had set up in their own honour following the custom of the Romans. The barrel vaults of the great warehouses may be seen in the quarters near the harbours. On the far side of the Golden Horn was the region of Galatea, where the farm land which surrounded the fortified settlement was given to soldiers who had retired from the army, but who could be called upon to fight if necessary.

HOUSES AND PALACES

In towns which developed from earlier settlements, people still lived in houses built in the Greek and Roman way. By the sixth century, houses of carefully-finished stone were to be found in Syria. At Refadeh the two-storeyed house, built to face a courtyard, had three rooms on the ground floor, two of which were connected by an archway. A covered walking way – *stoa* – ran along the front. On the opposite side of the courtyard, two towers were joined by a two-storeyed stoa, which, because it faced west, would have provided shade during the heat of the day. This house, standing on its own, must have been the property of a wealthy man. Town houses, usually built on either side of the straight streets, were entered through narrow doorways. On the ground floor was a large apartment spanned by an arch, and behind this was a stable with a ceiling of stone slabs, above which was another long room. The stable and room over were together the same height as the front apartment on the ground floor. The living quarters were on the first floor, reached by an outside stair. The flat roof was sometimes used by the occupants to catch the cool evening breezes. Where timber was more plentiful pitched roofs were used.

By the ninth century the Emperor, Leo the

*HOUSE, Medjdel,
S. Syria. A.D. 431.*

*HOUSE, Refadeh,
N. Syria. A.D. 516.*

*CHURCH AND PALACE,
Kasr ibn Wardan, N. Syria, A.D. 561–4.*

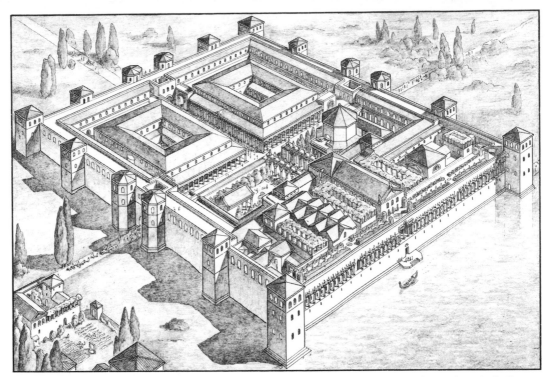

PALACE OF DIOCLETIAN, Split, Yugoslavia, late 3rd. C. A.D.

Wise, realised that planning was needed, and regulations were laid down. It was forbidden to build an oven or hearth in a party wall, that is, a common wall separating two dwellings, because fire might injure it. Citizens were required to keep their hay, rags and paper in unroofed, stonelined places to prevent fires. A man could not build a house in a position that would take away his neighbour's light. As in Ancient Rome, many people lived in blocks of flats, and it was an offence to throw water or slops out of the windows and so injure those below.

In the third century the Emperor Diocletian built a palace on the edge of the Adriatic Sea, where the town of Split now stands, much of it being actually inside the remains of the palace walls. The Golden Gate in the north wall opened on to a colonnaded road which ran south, with domestic quarters on either side. Beyond the crossing was a colonnaded court-yard leading to a domed vestibule opening into the Throne Room, behind which were the private apartments. Justinian's great palace of Constantinople (page 25, number 37) was described by Procopius as consisting of many buildings, needed to house the court officials and servants, who numbered several thousand. The main entrance was in the Forum Augustus, where a large archway led into the Chalke, or Brazen House, so called because its bronze doors and gilded roof tiles glittered in the sun. The emperor gave audiences in the Throne Room; steps of porphyry led up to the ivory and jewelled throne standing beneath a silver baldachino from which hung purple curtains that could be drawn when the emperor spoke with his ministers. Although this palace has disappeared, remains of the palace at Kasr ibn Wardan can still be seen. This palace unlike any other remains found in Syria closely resembles the plans and construction used in the imperial buildings of Justinian.

THE PALACE OF THEODORIC, A.D. 495–526, who became Emperor of the West by conquest and set up his capital at Ravenna, is shown in a mosaic on the wall of the church of S. Apollinare Nuovo. It illustrates a courtyard – *atrium* – such as might have been seen in front of the Throne Room in Diocletian's palace in Split. The central area was surrounded by arcades of round-headed arches supported on columns with Corinthian capitals. The abacus, the flat slab forming the top of the capital, had a rosette or cross carved on it. A large triple arch led into the Throne Room which was a basilica, probably similar in appearance to that at Trier (page 22). The plan of the Throne Room of the Great Palace of Constantinople, the *Chyrosotrikinlos*, was an exact copy of the church of S. Vitale in Ravenna (page 8).

During the winter months audiences were held inside, but in the warm summer weather they often took place in the courtyard. The Emperor, dressed in silk robes which glittered

with jewels and wearing a diadem on his head, was attended by leading church dignitaries and his principal ministers. The court ceremonial was laid down in every detail. If a man of importance wished to approach to make a request, he had to kneel before the ruler. The very lowest people were obliged to prostrate themselves, that is, lie flat on the ground before him with their arms outstretched. The reason for this was that the Byzantines believed that God had set the Emperor apart from ordinary men as a divine being; mosaics often show this idea by placing a nimbus behind the Emperor's head (see endpapers). As may be seen in the illustration, people from all parts of the Empire gathered in the palace. Some came to pursue law suits, others hoping to be noticed by the Emperor and given advancement. When Justinian was Emperor, so many people thronged to his palace that he made a special magistrate responsible for seeing that those whose business was finished returned to their homes.

HOSPITALS AND MONASTERIES

As Christians, the Byzantines were concerned with the care of the poor, the elderly and the sick. Hospitals and hostels were set up for them, sometimes attached to monasteries. In the infirmary – *zenon* – of the Monastery of the Pantocrator in Constantinople, there was a dispensary for medicines and an out-patients department, as well as fifty beds in five sections. A staff of sixty doctors, some of whom were women to deal with female patients, was employed to care for the sick; there were also nurses and orderlies. No expense was spared for the patients' comfort. They were given food and a little wine, and comfortable bedding was provided. Each ward had copper basins for the doctors to wash their hands in after they had finished work on a patient. At night time the wards and corridors were lighted, and a triple lamp was placed over the doctor's desk so that medicine and drugs could be dispensed with safety. Each hospital included a chapel, with priests assigned to it, where services were held for those who were well enough to attend. Other buildings included kitchens, a mill, a bakery, a laundry and stables.

In the very early days of Christianity a holy man would often find a cave or build a simple shelter where he could live a life of prayer. Gradually followers gathered around him to share his life. Each of them would live alone, but they would meet together for worship in the church. This form of community, known as a *lavra*, continued throughout the Byzantine period. However, as these monks were not subject to any discipline, some groups of monks also became organised under a *coen-*

HOSPITAL, BARLAAM MONASTERY,
Meteora, Greece. 16th. C.

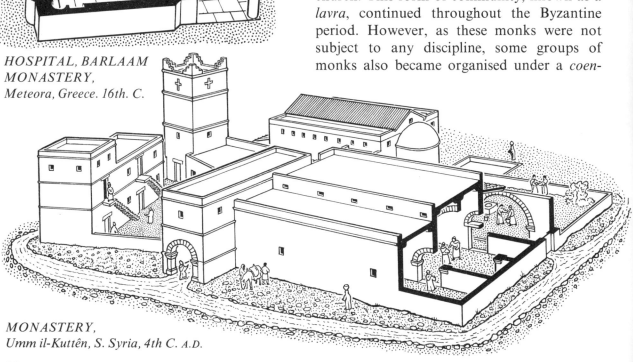

MONASTERY,
Umm il-Kuttên, S. Syria, 4th C. A.D.

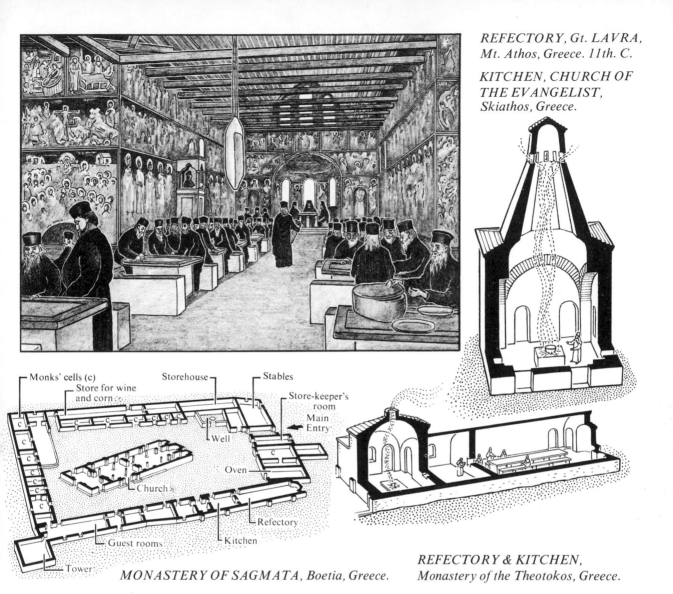

REFECTORY, Gt. LAVRA, Mt. Athos, Greece. 11th. C.

KITCHEN, CHURCH OF THE EVANGELIST, Skiathos, Greece.

MONASTERY OF SAGMATA, Boetia, Greece.

Monks' cells (c)
Store for wine and corn
Storehouse
Stables
Store-keeper's room
Main Entry
Well
Oven
Church
Refectory
Kitchen
Guest rooms
Tower

REFECTORY & KITCHEN, Monastery of the Theotokos, Greece.

obial system and buildings were needed for them. They lived together obeying a code of rules under the discipline of an abbot. The monastery, with a church in the middle of a courtyard, was surrounded by a high wall with only one door, guarded by an older monk. Against the inside of the walls were the monks' cells, storerooms and workshops. In addition to prayer, one of the monks' most important tasks was the copying and illuminating of manuscripts. Quarters were also set aside for pilgrims, travellers and the poor. The monks would meet for meals in the refectory, a long room with an apse at one end, where there was a reading desk to hold the book which was read aloud as the monks ate. They sat at a table which ran the length of the room with benches down either side, or at tables set into niches in the walls as may be seen above. The kitchen with its hearth was sometimes attached to the refectory, or, because of the risk of fire, was a separate building close by.

31

MARKETS.

The buying and selling of goods of all descriptions took place under the direct supervision of the state. Foreigners had their own quarters in Constantinople (page 25), where they bought and stored the luxury goods made by the Byzantines, which were eagerly sought after by wealthy men in Asia and Europe.

The quarters of the craftsmen, who made and sold goods, were to be found in great covered markets. These buildings, very like the markets of Rome, were built of brick and covered by barrel vaults or domes (see also *The Buildings of Early Islam*, pages 18–19). Here, as in all buildings with large domes or vaults, the builder was required by law to exercise skill and care to prevent weak foundations or crooked or uneven walls. If a building of this type collapsed within ten years, except by an Act of God such as an earthquake, the builder was required to replace it at his own expense.

Traders making and selling certain goods

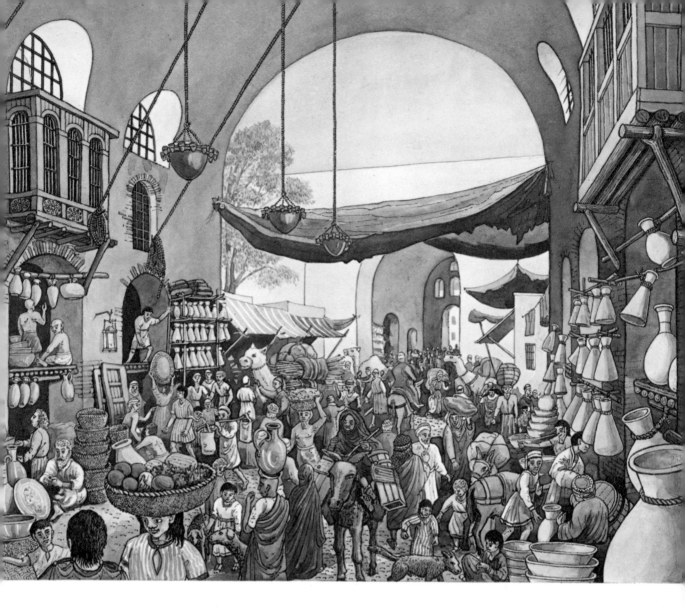

gathered together in their own quarters, as was the custom in Eastern Bazaars and also in the towns of medieval Europe. The jewellers and workers in enamel were to be found in one part of the market, while in another were the potters, and in yet another the sellers of silks. The craftsmen's workshops were set behind open arches, in front of which goods were displayed and the merchants stood calling their wares to encourage people to buy. State officials mingled with the crowds to see that the correct prices were charged. A merchant caught cheating and raising the agreed price could be fined. The family lived over the workshop, reaching their quarters by means of wooden ladders set up at the back of the premises. This made the most use of the available space, the floors of this upper level resting on timber beams. Daylight came into the building through the open ends and from openings set high up in the walls; at night oil lamps hanging from great chains lit the scene.

Left: Dancer, from an
11th. C. manuscript.

Right: Scene from
an ivory reliquary.
c. A.D. 370.

ENTERTAINMENT AND INNS

In Constantinople the Hippodrome, similar to that of Ancient Rome, had seating for some forty thousand spectators to watch the chariot racing. Displays of wrestling, mimes and dancing took place between the races. Fights between gladiators, such as might have been seen in Rome, were not permitted. The ivory casket (above) shows a theatrical arrangement which may have been the forerunner of a type of staging used in the presentation of Miracle and Morality plays in medieval Europe.

Inns were built to lodge the many people who thronged the cities. In Syria, the larger ones were two-storeyed with an open stoa in front. The space inside was divided up into large rooms, each with a row of mangers set across one end to form a stable, so that a man could keep an eye on his animals.

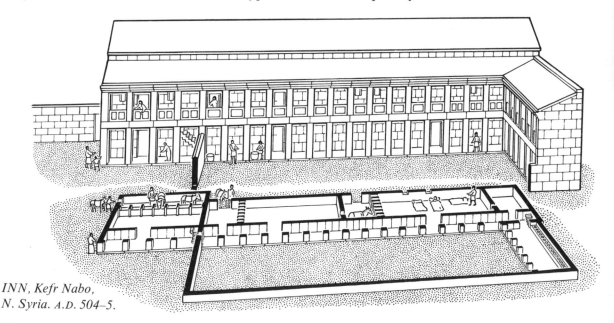

INN, Kefr Nabo,
N. Syria. A.D. 504–5.

FORTRESS, Der il-Kahf,
N. Syria. A.D. *367–375.*

FARMHOUSE,
Gasr Duib, Tripolitania.
c. A.D. *244–6.*

FORTIFICATIONS

To protect the great caravan routes of the Empire, Justinian set up chains of small forts. These had only one gate which was protected by towers; the surrounding walls were about twenty-five feet (7.62 metres) high and were sometimes as thick as ten feet (3.048 metres). The living quarters were placed against the inner face of the wall, and in the middle of the courtyard there was often a church. In addition to such military outposts, farmers in outlying areas built fortified farmhouses, many of which followed the pattern used earlier by the Romans. One entrance in the strong, windowless, walls led to a courtyard around which were the rooms. Wooden stairs led to an upper storey where all the rooms opened off each other, only one door giving access to the stairs. Lookout towers might be one or two storeys.

THE BLACK TOWER,
Rimeli Hisar,
Constantinople.
A.D. *1100.*

From the late seventh century Byzantium and Islam were continuously at war with each other; it is not surprising therefore to find many similar features in their fortifications. Outlying works controlling the Bosphorus had been built from the earliest times. The Black Tower (page 35) has been reconstructed to show what it looked like in Byzantine times. Used as a fortress and a prison, it was known as one of the towers of Lethe or oblivion, as little light reached the interior. In 1454 the Turks added two further storeys to the top of the tower.

Constantine had built sea-walls around the peninsula and across the neck of land to enclose his capital. However, during the reign of Theodosius II, A.D. 408–450, a further wall (above and page 24, no. 1) was built on the landward side to accommodate the growing city. This new wall was about thirty feet (9.144 metres) high, sixteen feet (4.87 metres) thick and some four and a half miles (7.24 kilometres) in length. The wall had six gates

leading into the city and ninety-six towers projecting from it. It was constructed of concrete faced with small limestone blocks and reinforced at intervals by bands of five courses of thin bricks set in thick beds of mortar. In front of the main wall was an advance wall, the two being separated by a moat sixty feet (18.28 metres) wide. Outside the advance wall was an embankment and broad ditch. This was the first time that the use of two walls as a means of fortification had been employed.

The invention in the early seventh century of 'Greek Fire', a mixture which was inflammable even under water, had saved Constantinople from the attacks of the Arabs when they blockaded the city from A.D. 655 to 677. This fire could be thrown by catapults, and later a type of rocket tube was used to propel it.

It was, however, Christians from the west who sacked the city in the Fourth Crusade in 1204. Many of the churches and rich palaces were burnt and plundered by the Crusaders.

IVORY VIRGIN
from 10th. C.
Triptych.

After the fall of the capital, the rest of the Empire was divided among the various countries that had taken part in the Crusade. In 1261, however, the conquerors were put to flight and a new emperor was acclaimed in Constantinople. The Empire managed to exist for another two hundred years, but it was never again to become a great power. Danger from the east was a constant threat. During the thirteenth century the Turks had captured most of Asia Minor and then turned towards Europe. Finally Constantinople was encircled by conquered territories, and on 29 May, 1453, the city fell to the Turkish Army of Mehmet II.

Many Byzantine churches were turned into mosques, and this is one reason why so many have survived. Hagia Sophia itself became a mosque, but today it has been turned into a museum where it is possible to see both Christian and Islamic religious architecture side by side. Turkish home life was very different from that of the Byzantines, so most of the dwelling houses were allowed to decay and fall into ruins.

The fall of the Byzantine Empire had an unexpected effect on Europe. Scholars who possessed priceless manuscripts, many written before the birth of Christ, fled to the west. So it was that the ideas of the Ancient Greeks and Romans became known once more. The rebirth of these ideas, known as the New Learning, caused men to start thinking for themselves, and led to the period called the Renaissance when modern scientific thought was born.

ACKNOWLEDGEMENTS

The authors wish to thank M. E. Martin, R. J. Hopper and the librarians of Leicester Polytechnic, the Barber Institute and the school of Oriental and African Studies of the University of London for their invaluable help. They would also like to thank the authors of the many books which have formed the background to this study, including: Abbate, F., *Christian Art,* London, 1972; Baynes, N. H. and Moss, H. St. L. B., *Byzantium,* Oxford, 1961; Beckwith, J., *The Art of Constantinople,* London, 1961; Bovini, G., *Ravenna Mosaics,* London; Boyle, L., *St Clement's, Rome,* Rome, 1963; Browning, R., *Justinian and Theodora,* London, 1971; Butler, H. C., *Ancient Architecture in Syria,* sects. A & B, Leyden, 1907–21; Codellas, P. S., *The Pantocrator,* Bulletin of the History of Medicine, xii, 1942; Constantelos, D., *Byzantine Philanthropy and Social Welfare,* New Brunswick, 1968; Goodchild, R. G., *The Limes Tripolitanus II,* Journal of Roman Studies, xl, 1950; Gough, M., *The Origins of Christian Art,* London, 1973; Grabar, A., *Byzantium,* London, 1966; Hamilton, J. A., *Byzantine Architecture and Decoration,* London, 1933; Haussig, H. W., *A History of Byzantine Civilization,* London, 1971; Haynes, D. E. L., *The Antiquities of Tripolitania,* Libya, 1959; Hearsey, J. E. N., *City of Constantinople,* London, 1963; Jones, A. H. M., *The Decline of the Ancient World,* London, 1968; Kostof, S. K., *Orthodox Baptistery of Ravenna,* Yale, 1965; Krautheimar, R., *Early Christian and Byzantine Architecture,* London, 1975; Lassus, J., *The Early Christian and Byzantine World,* London, 1966; Lethaby, W. R. and Swainson, H., *The Church of Sancta Sophia,* London, 1894; Macdonald, W. L., *Early Christian and Byzantine Achitecture,* New York, 1962; Mesini, G., *Ravenna,* Ravenna, 1961; Millet, G., *Monuments Byzantine de Mistra,* Paris, 1910; Orlandos, A. K., *Monastiriaki Architektoniki,* Athens, 1926; *Monastery of Sagmata,* Archeion, vii, 1951; Reusch, W., *Die Basilika in Trier,* Trier, 1956; Rice, D. T., *Art of the Byzantine Era,* London, 1963; *Byzantine Art,* Harmondsworth, 1968; *Monasteries of Mt Athos,* Antiquity, vol. 2, 1928; Rostoutzeff, M., *Dura-Europos and its Art,* Oxford, 1938; Schneider, A. M. and Karnapp, W., *Die Stadtmauer von Iznik (Nicaea),* Berlin, 1938; Schneider, A. M., *The City Walls of Istanbul,* Antiquity, vol. xi, 1937; Sherrard, P., *Constantinople,* London, 1965; Stern, H., *Santa Constanza,* Dumbarton Oaks Papers, vol. 12, Washington, 1958; Stewart. A., *Procopius, Of the Buildings of Justinian,* London, 1886; Stewart, C., *The Great Palace of the Byzantine Emperors,* London, 1947; Toy, S., *The Castles of the Bosphorus,* Archaelogia, vol. lxxx, 1930; West, A., *All about the Crusades,* London, 1967.

THE BYZANTINE EMPIRE *in the time of Justinian.*

Trier · Périgueux · GALLIA · HISPANIA · DALMATIA · DACIA · PONTUS EUXINUS · THRACIA · MACEDONIA · PONTUS · ITALIA · ASIA · CAPPODOCIA · NUMIDIA · AFRICA PROCONSULARIS · SICILIA · GREECE · CYPRUS · Dura-Europos · SYRIA · MEDITERRANEAN SEA · TRIPOLITANIA · LIBYA · EGYPT

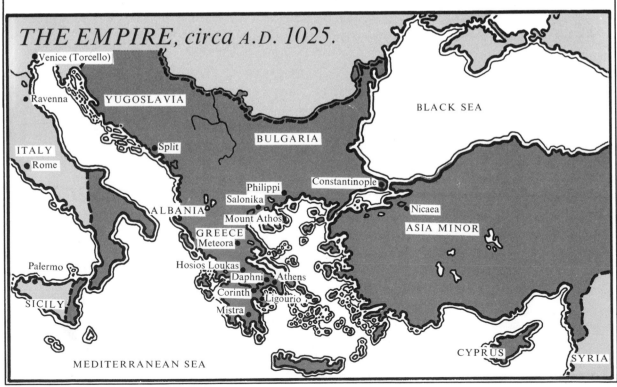

THE EMPIRE, *circa A.D. 1025.*

Venice (Torcello) · Ravenna · YUGOSLAVIA · Split · BULGARIA · BLACK SEA · ITALY · Rome · Philippi · Constantinople · Salonika · ALBANIA · Mount Athos · Nicaea · GREECE · Meteora · ASIA MINOR · Palermo · Hosios Loukas · Daphni · Athens · Corinth · Ligourio · SICILY · Mistra · CYPRUS · SYRIA · MEDITERRANEAN SEA

*THE PANTANASSA,
Mistra, Greece. 15th. C.*

Books by Helen and Richard Leacroft

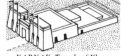

THE BUILDINGS OF ANCIENT EGYPT

KARNAK, Temple of Khons

". . . well written and authoritative and covers much in the way of social history. No other juvenile book covering ancient Egypt gives anything comparable to these informative illustrations. . . . Meets curriculum requests for material on architecture of homes through the ages." *Library Journal*

THE BUILDINGS OF ANCIENT MESOPOTAMIA

BABYLON, Ishtar Gate

". . . The text is clear and efficient. . . . The diagrams are clear, well labelled, and closely fitted to the text. The drawings are also clear and evocative, and the colour spreads are impressive. . . . The publishers must be congratulated on using every square inch of space, end-papers, covers and all, yet without giving the book a cluttered appearance." *The Junior Bookshelf*

THE BUILDINGS OF ANCIENT ROME

NIMES, Maison Carrée

"Should be in every school library, if not in every classroom." *School Librarian*
"It is easy to become absorbed in the past, and the Leacrofts present an enticing opportunity to indulge. The superb illustrations of Roman public and private buildings spark the imagination. They lead one to reconstruct the lives of the people. With scrupulous attention to detail the Leacrofts depict the Romans' technological inventiveness, peerless practicality, and adaptive skill . . . its pages are packed with information." *Christian Teacher*

THE BUILDINGS OF ANCIENT MAN

STONEHENGE

"The text . . . is once again interesting and informative and includes clear explanations of many archaeological and technical terms. This would be a good introduction to the subject for people of nine and upwards." *The Times Educational Supplement*
"The text is well written . . . informative illustrations, many of which are in full color . . . this book is excellent for its information on early buildings and their construction." *School Library Journal*

THE BUILDINGS OF ANCIENT GREECE

ATHENS, The Parthenon

"It could scarcely be better as a library reference for imaginative and recreative work by the pupils." *The Teacher*
"An informative text complements the excellent illustrations on every page which consists of interpretations of Greek life, mostly in color and precise, carefully labelled drawings showing architectural details. Like the Leacrofts' THE BUILDINGS OF ANCIENT EGYPT . . . valuable in the study of a civilization and of architecture in general." *The Booklist* (*American Library Association*)

THE BUILDINGS OF EARLY ISLAM

BURSA, Mosque of Alaeddin Bey

"The illustrations are clear and informative, covering every surface including the serviceable strong binding. The excellent text makes this a fascinating source book which must surely catch the interest of the reader and provide a comprehensive base from which to explore further a culture and civilisation which has had such an impact on Western Europe." *The Junior Bookshelf*

ABOUT THE AUTHORS

Richard Leacroft trained as an architect and scene designer and is now Principal Lecturer in the School of Architecture, Leicester Polytechnic where he teaches the history of architecture. Helen Leacroft trained as an actress at RADA, but later turned to teaching, and is now Deputy Headmistress of a secondary school.

Mosaic decoration from the
Great Palace at Constantinople.

The Last Supper : mosaic from
S. Apollinare Nuovo, Ravenna.

Duck : mosaic from
the Church of the
Multiplication, Tabgah.

Charioteer
from Lampadius' dipty

Empress Theodora :
from S. Vitale,
Ravenna.

The healing of the
paralysed man, seen
carrying his bed :
a mosaic from
S. Apollinare Nuovo.

Cupids fishin
mosaic from
Aquileia.

Ox cart : mosaic
from S. Constanza,
Rome.

Duck : mosaic from
the Church of the
Multiplication,
Tabgah.

Mosaic from S. Apollinare
Nuovo, Ravenna, Italy.